SAYING "YES"

A Pastor's Journal

*"For as many as may be the promises of God,
in Him they are yes..."*
(2 Corinthians 1:20a)

Bob Yawberg

© Copyright 2019 by Bob Yawberg

All rights reserved. No part of this publication may be reproduced, stored in a retrieval system, or transmitted in any form or by any means—electronic, mechanical, photocopying, recording, or otherwise—without the prior written permission of the publisher and copyright owner. The only exception is brief quotations in printed reviews.

The views expressed in this book are the author's and do not necessarily reflect those of the publisher.

Published in the United States of America

7710-T Cherry Park Dr, Ste 224

Houston, TX 77095

(713) 766-4271

ISBN: 978-0-578-43461-2

CONTENTS

1 CRISIS OF FAITH 7
2 58 YEARS AND COUNTING 11
3 LIFETIME WARRANTY 15
4 WE PROMISED 17
5 SECOND-HAND DESK 19
6 SHOW UP AND SHUT UP 21
7 WORDS TO PONDER 23
8 JESUS, STILL THE ANSWER 25
9 "READY KILOWATT" 26
10 THE CHOICE 29
11 HOMEBLIND 31
12 REPENTANCE LEADS TO CONFESSION 33
13 A MAN OF COLOR 35
14 SILENCE 37
15 SCOTCH TAPE AND SCISSORS 39
16 FAMILY 41
17 PREACHERS AS PERSUADERS 43
18 THE ONLY RELIGION WITH A CROSS! 45
19 PRAYER MEANS EVERYTHING 47
20 DAYS OF PRAYER 49
21 PARENTING IS TEMPORARY 53
22 ON RETREAT 55
23 WORTH THE WAIT! 57
24 I PULLED THE WEED 59

27	WHY DADDY, WHY?	61
28	LEAD GENTLY	63
27	MY DAD TAUGHT ME	65
28	WORSHIP STYLE	67
29	MILKWEED PODS IN THE WIND	69
30	SOLITUDE	71
31	REPENTANCE AND HOLINESS	73
32	URGENT OR IMPORTANT	75
33	DISCIPLE-MAKING	77
34	SECOND SOPRANO	79
35	THE TIGHTROPE WALKER	81
36	SHORTER PRAYERS	83
37	DISCIPLESHIP IN TWO YEARS	84
38	BELOVED SUFFERER	87
39	FROM FOUNTAIN PEN TO COMPUTER	89
40	"SOUL OF CHRIST"	91

East window, Broadway Christian Church,
"Behold, I stand at the door and knock."

1
CRISIS OF FAITH

1951 Fall - (Oberlin College - age 18, Freshman) I am not sure I can make it! Attending German classes six mornings a week at 7:00 a.m. It looks like I may have to drop "Mien Deutz." Our German professor is merciless. I have gotten no letter from Marilyn today; I will probably get two tomorrow because she never fails to send one. Then tonight, a fellow freshman from nearby Cleveland stopped by my room. He spied my Bible. I can still hear his laughter as he turned and walked down the hall. "Do you believe every word of that old book? Every word?"

I've never been challenged like that. Do I believe? I've been taught all my life that everything in this Book is true. Do I believe that because my parents believe as well? I'm pre-enrolled in Seminary to become a preacher. Then just before bed, I listened to my nightly radio program from the local Four Square Church. Upon hearing their theme song, "It is No Secret What God Can do," I sensed the Lord's presence. Yes, I want to believe, I must believe, but do I?

2011-April 7 - REFLECTION - That night, in the men's building room #400, my faith was severely tested. The ensuing year brought more questions. I audited an NT seminary class. The professor teaching seminary students claimed, "Jesus never walked on water, only a sandbar. Peter fell into a hole! There was no miracle of Jesus feeding 5,000 people; they merely shared their lunches." That year of questioning led to a deep and real personal faith and conviction, Yes, Yes, I believe Jesus! He believed the Scriptures he learned as a child. He believed, and that's enough for me. The words of the nightly theme song on my old Emerson radio gave me hope.

"The chimes of Time ring out the news;

Another day is through;

Someone slipped and fell;

Was that someone you?

You may have longed for added strength;

Your courage to renew;

Do not be disheartened,

For I bring hope to you."

"It's no secret what God can do;

What He's done for others,

He'll do for you.

With arms wide open,

He'll pardon you.

It is no secret what God can do!"

- Stuart Hamblin

"God means what he says. What he says goes. His powerful Word is sharp as a surgeon's scalpel, cutting through everything, whether doubt or defense, laying us open to listen and obey. Nothing and no one is impervious to God's Word. We can't get away from it---no matter what." **Hebrews 4:12 (MSG)**

2
58 YEARS AND COUNTING

1953 February 24-JOURNAL ENTRY- I have just returned from the Methodist Church in Bowling Green, Ohio after talking with my District Superintendent. Now that I have my Local Preacher's License, I asked for permission to answer a call from the Neapolis Church of Christ in my hometown. He consented and thought it a very good opportunity to gain experience and also to help the people there. This is the day I've anticipated for a long time! The start to making disciples as a pastor. I've prayed to God, and I am so happy that I can hardly restrain myself. I want to tell the world I have a church and can, at last, serve my Lord as a Christian minister. I only hope and pray to remain humble, so I always look to Almighty God for supreme help and guidance.

2/25 (The next day) – I have just now received the second answer to my prayer in the last 24 hours. Marilyn wrote, telling me how she has found the love of God in her heart and wants to help me in my call to ministry. My heart is leaping for joy; what more could happen or what more could I ask for?

2011-March 3 – REFLECTION - The above was recorded by pen and ink in my journal, beginning in September of 1952, while I was a junior at BGSU. 58 years ago, on the 1st of March which was a Sunday, the Neapolis

Church elders called me to preach. It would be a temporary arrangement until they could find a more experienced man from their fellowship of churches. We agreed on $10.00 a week, as that amount came in.

I would not turn 20 until the end of March. Marilyn and I would be married the following November. We could never have chosen a life work to compare with the call God gave us in 1953. Little could we have imagined what lay ahead. There would be graduate work at the Cincinnati Bible Seminary, where I traveled by train to attend my classes four days a week. It meant leaving Marilyn and our baby son every Monday evening. Two years later, to obtain more coursework, I traveled by Greyhound Bus to the Butler School of Religion in Indianapolis, attending classes two days a week.

We assumed our work in Neapolis would be temporary. However, the Lord kept us there for 11 years. During that first decade of ministry, I learned to preach by preaching, pastor by pastoring, and most of all, the vital role of prayer undergirding all we attempted.

> *"I've preached you to the whole congregation,*
> *I've kept back nothing, God – You know that.*
> *I didn't keep the news of your ways;*
> *A secret, didn't keep it to myself.*
> *I told it all, how dependable you are, how*
> *thorough. I didn't hold back pieces*
> *of love and truth."*
> **Psalm 40:10 (MSG)**

Bob, his father, Fred, and '37 Willys

3
LIFETIME WARRANTY

1953-JOURNAL ENTRY- Saturday, was a day Marilyn and I will never forget! Two of our dreams came true. First, Dad loaned money for a deep blue, 4-door '49 Plymouth. Later, I drove Marilyn downtown to pick out her engagement ring. It doesn't seem possible; it's like a dream. The local jeweler, our good friend, sold it for $140.00, including the wedding ring. We've saved dimes during our high school dating years, so we had most of it. Back to Marilyn's house, I typed my sermon after drinking three cups of coffee to stay awake.

It was Sunday morning and my 20th birthday. It was hard to concentrate on all my duties (with Marilyn sitting in the front row) and the car outside in the parking lot. It was time to preach my sermon, "Christian Enthusiasm." I was so happy. I'll never regret my decision to marry my beloved and enter the Christian ministry.

2011 March – REFLECTION - Cars often occupy a young man's fancy. Dad gave me my first one at 16, his old '37 Willys. Years later, the Willys and the '49 Plymouth were laid to rest in a junkyard. However, Marilyn still wears the small diamond in her wedding ring.

Exchanging rings at our wedding included the promise to love each other till death. That promise came with a lifetime warranty! The most important things in life are not what we purchase but who we are.

> Paul writes, *"Go after a life of love, as if your life depended on it – because it does!"* **1 Cor. 14:1 (MSG)**

Bob and Marilyn, November 21, 1953

4
WE PROMISED

1953 November-JOURNAL ENTRY- (Two days before our wedding). The past three days have been wonderful. I've never been so happy! A big smile is on my face everywhere I go. Whistling as I walk down the street, I think of my dearest wife to be and the life we are going to live.

How could I feel any different? Marilyn is the most perfect girl I've ever known. A sparkling personality with physical beauty, and above all, a sincere belief in God and desire for His work. Together, our life can't help but be successful. We'll never be rich financially, but we'll be happy in God's service — something all the money in the world cannot buy.

2007 November – REFLECTION - We met at church when Marilyn was 12 and I, 14. We were drawn to one another even then. 54 years ago, we were married. I at 20, a junior at Bowling Green State University had begun preaching eight months earlier. Marilyn at 18, graduated from High School that spring and worked at the University Book Store.

Last week, a neighbor asked, "What is the secret to staying married that long?" I replied, "We promised... for better or worse, for richer or poorer, in sickness and health, to love and cherish till death do us part." Life rotated between "better or worse," and the poorer came before the richer. I would be ill often, but she always saw me back to health. Moreover, we have been blessed with the legacy of our parents who were married, when combined, for a total of 112 years.

We found life in ministry both fulfilling and demanding. Life is like that, no matter the nature of your work. The grace of our Lord Jesus combined with the prayers of many have made it possible to begin our 55th year. All praise to Almighty God!

> *"An excellent wife who can find? For her worth is far above jewels. The heart of her husband trusts in her, and he will have no lack of gain."* **Prov. 31:10-11 (NASB)**

5
SECOND-HAND DESK

1954 January-JOURNAL ENTRY- Junior at Bowling Green State University, age 20. On a Tuesday, I just got one of my Geology papers back, and I failed it! I spent more than eight hours working on that essay, but I received only a C+. I failed my German test as well. Things are tough.

I was doing too much that semester, with my church in Neapolis, Ohio and getting married (that was enough in itself). I never had enough time to do all I should at church, let alone school. The church was doing well. We averaged about 100 the previous month. More important than attendance is spiritual progress. It is my hope and prayer that people would increase in this too. I must have a better attitude now than when I first began.

I bought a secondhand desk, twelve dollars at the used-furniture store in Bowling Green. It means so much to have a desk of my own. It's been a long day, and we're both tired; it's time to turn in.

I finished a chapter in A.W. Tozer's *Pursuit of God*. He wrote of the low religious plane we are living on today. I wholeheartedly agree! We've tried to use our gadgets in connection with God. We've tried to squeeze a few minutes out of our busy schedule for Him. How true, in my own life especially.

2010 June – REFLECTION - The above was written 56 years ago. Little has changed since then. Gadgets have turned into computers, Blackberries, cell phones, and iPods. A desk is still a desk, filled with even more busy work. What promised to save time suddenly demands more of our time. Are we slaves to technology?

Tozer seems ever applicable. God often receives our leftovers. Spiritual progress eludes us. How timely are Jesus' words, *"Blessed are those who hunger and thirst for righteousness, for they shall be satisfied."* Matt. 5:6 (NASB)

Lord, stir in me a huge appetite for spiritual nutrition. Only You, Your ways, Your Word and Your promises ultimately satisfy.

6
SHOW UP AND SHUT UP

1954 JOURNAL ENTRY- The early years are the most. Little did I realize how much my life and future would be affected by a 34-year old preacher from Toledo, Ohio, 30 miles north of where I began ministry. He was married, a father of four children, and leading a growing congregation.

T. W. Overton took time from an already full schedule to listen to a bewildered preacher boy from the country. We talked for nearly two hours. He then took me to lunch; all the corned beef we could eat. This was the beginning of a relationship that would last until he died.

2009 July – REFLECTION - What took place in 1954 is now known today as "mentoring." This word was not in my vocabulary then. It most certainly is now, as some younger men look to me on a regular basis for encouragement and insight. It is my prayer that I am available to them as Tommy Overton was to me the day I stopped at his study, unannounced. In 1978, he flew from Huntington Beach, CA, to preach at our twenty-fifth ministry/marriage anniversary.

Eugene Peterson speaks about "spiritual directors" in an interview with *Christian Century:*

(March 13, 2002) "I have two basic definitions; one is to show up then shut up. It's important that people have a place they can come to and know you're going to be there with and for them. The other is that spiritual direction largely involves what you do when you don't think you're doing anything. You aren't trying to solve a problem, and occasionally, it might seem like you're not making a difference. Be patient. It takes a lot of restraint and discipline for a pastor not to say anything, not do anything. But the pastoral school is an ideal school for learning how to."

> *"Instruct them in the practice of all I have commanded you. I'll be with you as you do this, day after day, right up to the end of the age."* **Matt. 28:20 (MSG)**

Great-grandson, Henry

7
WORDS TO PONDER

1956 August-JOURNAL ENTRY- Attending Standard Publishing's Conference on Christian Education was my first visit to Cincinnati. Several older preachers invited me to lunch at the Plaza Cafeteria in the basement of the newest and largest hotel in the city. I ordered, following their example, Sirloin Tip cooked to order plus several side dishes. $2.09! Twice as much as I should have paid. I felt ashamed, spending the Lord's money on such luxury. The church folk gave me $45 to cover the entire week's expense.

After lunch, I accepted an invitation to their hotel, the Sheraton Gibson. Another beautiful and almost lavish place. Their room had a private bath and a TV. Later, I had my shoes half-soled, new heels, and a sparkling shine; shoes like new for $3.50.

Quite a contrast with my stay at the Cincinnati Bible Seminary dorm where I'll be rooming this fall. I think I like it better. Is it right or good for us to have so much luxury? We must beware of becoming soft and complacent. It seems in the future we could by God's grace go on to a large city church, but is that best? The small ones need help too, and we prefer the small town or even the country where I grew up. May God's will be done.

2011 September – REFLECTION - How does one apply the words of Jesus today as He sent His twelve harvest hands with this charge?

> *"Don't think you have to put on a fund-raising campaign before you start. You don't need a lot of equipment. You are the equipment… travel light. When you enter a town or village, don't insist on staying in a luxury inn. Get a modest place with some modest people, and be content there until you leave."* Matt.10:9-11 (MSG)

East window Broadway Christian Church, "I am the way, and the truth, and the life."

8
JESUS, STILL THE ANSWER

1960 Summer-JOURNAL ENTRY- On vacation at Clear Lake, Indiana. People are so wrapped up in powerboats, drinking parties, fine homes, and appearance management! The real value, quality, and zest of life escapes them. How ironic to see people pursuing an ideal of happiness by empty purses and burning the candle of life at both ends. Like a 4th of July Roman Candle, a momentary brilliant light flashing, but then darkness, darker than before.

This morning, as I rocked our three-month-old daughter, I looked out over the lake, and a question occurred to me: "What is reality?" We live in a critical period of conflicting ideologies and power. Where can we find the final, uncompromising answer to the truth?

John, the Apostle, claims it to be in the person of One Jesus Christ of Nazareth. In his first chapter, he proclaims Christ. Christ alone quenches thirst and is food to fulfill all hunger and peace to pacify the most troubled mind. In this year of 1960, Christ is the answer!

2011 January – REFLECTION - We've lived long enough to test the Christ answer. However, we must connect the record of the Bible to life and power. The reality of Christ Jesus, He is present now, not just then. He not only once lived, but He lives today as men and women claim Him as Lord of their lives. We will soon mark our 58th year of ministry. The closer we come to the end of this life, the more convinced we are of Jesus Christ and His crucifixion. He is truth! He does give life. There is none like Him!

> *"The Life-Light blazed out of darkness; the darkness couldn't put it out.*
>
> *The Word became flesh and blood, and moved into our neighborhood."* **John 1:5, 14 (MSG)**

Frozen Lake Erie in January

9
"READY KILOWATT"

1962 September-JOURNAL ENTRY- All is dark from a severe electrical storm. I am sitting at the kitchen table writing by candlelight. How dependent we are upon the little god of modern living, "Ready Kilowatt!" (For six decades, a fictional spokesman for the electrical industry.)

There are no lights on the street. Our six-year-old son is worried because the only light in his room is coming from a strangely dim, flickering candle. Yes, God has again shown the force of nature can stop man in his tracks. Frig is still, no pump for water, the furnace cold, and our fancy bathroom fixtures worthless.

2017 September – REFLECTION - Just as we were dependent on our utilities 55 years ago, it is no different now. Vivid reminders this past month with the devastation caused by hurricane Irma. Were the entire nation's power grid to go down, it is likely that for a lengthy period we would experience life as the early church. Then people went to bed and arose with the sun. They lived with no air conditioning, refrigeration, food from supermarkets shelves, and modern technology.

By God's grace, we flew to Fort Wayne, Indiana, on September 3rd for a Pastors In Prayer Board meeting and retreat. On the day we were scheduled to return, Irma struck.

We spent the next three weeks with our daughter and loving family waiting for power. Thank You, Lord, there was no serious damage. Sobering times demand *rethinking* and *reevaluating*. Could it be, "Less is more."

> **"Give your entire attention to what God is doing right now, and don't get worked up about what may or may not happen tomorrow. God will help you deal with whatever hard things come up when the time comes."** Matt. 6:34 (MSG)

10
THE CHOICE

I said, "Let me walk in the fields;"
He said, "No, walk in the town;"
I said, "There are no flowers there;"
"No flowers, "He said, "But a crown."

I said, "But the sky is black,
And there's nothing but noise and din;"
But He wept as He sent me back;
"There is more, there is sin."

I said, "But the air is thick,
And fogs are veiling the sun;"
He answered, "Yet hearts are sick,
And souls in the dark undone."

I said, "I shall miss the light,
And friends will miss me," they say.
He answered me, "Choose tonight
If I am to miss you or them."

I pleaded for time to be given;
He said, "Is it hard to decide?
It will not seem hard in heaven
To have followed the steps of your guide."

I cast one look at the field,

Then set my face to the town;
He said, "My child, do you yield?
Will you leave the flowers for the crown?"

Then into His hand went mine,
And into my heart came He,
Now I walk in a light divine;
The path I had feared to see!

Yawberg family homestead

11
HOMEBLIND

1967 APRIL – JOURNAL ENTRY - Today, a startling realization hit me! Our son has already been with us for more than half the years of his childhood and our daughter over one-third of hers. As I walked down our street on Putnam, I enjoyed balmy spring temperatures with a touch of lilac in the air. It made me realize that this is the home they will remember. We need more time together to listen, talk, read and play.

Suddenly, I'm overcome with the terrific pace we've been keeping since our return from vacation. Tonight, it will be good to sit for an hour, to stop and think and realize how great the opportunities surrounding us are.

2018 JUNE 1 – REFLECTION – "The life not reflected upon is not worth living." A little boy sought his father's attention as the dad buried his face behind the Sports page. "Listen to me, Daddy!" He cried. "I am listening, son!" "No, Daddy, I want you to listen with your eyes."

Mike Napa writes, "How could you be blind to something you look at a dozen times a day?" Social scientists call it being "homeblind." Commonplace details fail to register; we become blind to the familiar.

Looking back over a lifetime of ministry, I redefine success as being respected by those who know me best — my family. There is no greater honor or privilege that any man can ever hope to have.

> *"Finish what You started in me, God. Your love is eternal – don't quit on me now."*
> **Psalm 138 (MSG)**

Bob, early childhood

12
REPENTANCE LEADS TO CONFESSION

1967 September (Age 37)- JOURNAL ENTRY- After breakfast, I felt a deep hunger to pray. Entering a small room off the balcony, I locked the door and spent one full hour with the Lord. At times, I was on my knees, other times pacing up and down, back and forth. Then standing before the window overlooking our city, "Lord, what do You want with my life?"

I have been losing purpose and direction. There is never enough time to study. My devotional life is sorely wanting, just a brief prayer as I go. My bible sessions are now done on an irregular basis. The joy and satisfaction of serving Christ replaced by pressure, meetings, and schedules. Am I trying to build a personal reputation? People compliment me, and soon I get the idea that it is "my" ministry, forgetting the Lord's call to work for HIM.

On my knees again, "Lord, whatever Your will is for me, I accept. I'm through with "my" ministry; I want to make it yours. I've cared too much about pleasing men. Now I want to please You." I also wrote on the flyleaf of my Bible, "May God help me keep this resolve as I return to the world with all its allure and illusion."

2016 March (Age 82) – REFLECTION (Nearly 50 years later) - The resolve faded, but it was still readable. I've since realized that God wants my repentance. Repentance leads to confession, one of the spiritual disciplines. "Confession is an action by which we do what we can to receive from God the ability or power to do what we cannot by our own effort." Spiritual Formation Bible

Thomas Merton once wrote, "My relationship with God needs constant renewal. I pray what is lukewarm will spring into living flame. What is dry will become living water. What is deaf and blind will return to light and life." Thomas Merton. That is my prayer for you, my reader, as well.

"The zeal of the Lord of hosts shall accomplish this." **Isaiah 9:7 (MSG)**

13
A MAN OF COLOR

1967 - JOURNAL ENTRY – Recently, a black man and his wife were called to Fort Wayne, Indiana, to start an inner-city ministry. Having recently moved from a rural community, my experience with other races was limited if non-existent. Major change lay just ahead.

Sometime after Sam and Arvina Winger arrived, he and I stood on a downtown street corner praying. Sam began, "Lord if someone talks about Bob, they are talking about Sam." And I prayed likewise, "Lord if someone talks about Sam, they are talking about Bob." Neither of us realized then where those prayers would take us.

Three years later, a fellow pastor came to Sam and made accusations against me. Sam replied, "Have you talked to Bob? I have nothing to say until you talk to Bob and get your answer from him."

2002 July – REFLECTION - When we pray and act upon what we prayed, we can expect results! Our Lord cares deeply for the broken, grieving and forsaken who live not far from us. Not until I met a man of color, and prayed with him, did my vision and heart change. Looking back, I realize that we do not make friends in the middle of a crisis, we make friends long beforehand. George W. Bush once noted, "Too often we judge other groups by their worst example while we judge ourselves by our best intentions."

"Let Me give you a new command... This is how everyone will recognize that you are my disciples — when they see the love you have for one another." **John 13:34-35 (MSG)**

14
SILENCE

1968 October-JOURNAL ENTRY- Reading Theilicke's *Encounter with Spurgeon*:

> "We preach peace and radiate restlessness. We are perpetual producers, worshipping the gods of production, which is why the valley of dry bones spreads all around us. A detour to quiet and stillness is needed. We must read the Bible as nourishment for our soul. The light we let shine before men is borrowed light, a mere reflection."

To this, I agree.

2018 MAY 18 – REFLECTION - I yearn for silence. All we do becomes a pulsating, forceful drive., surrounded by sirens, TV, Internet, and iPhones. We need background melodies at the Mall while the band plays on, even during the Lord's Supper.

Sitting on the front porch of my boyhood home by rural Jeffers Road, we were surrounded by silence. On a warm summer night, I would lay in the hammock, with Mom and Dad nearby. The only sounds recalled were crickets and the Whip-poor-will calling to his mate.

Nostalgia? Am I becoming an "Old Timer" who idealizes memories of another day? Where do I fit in the present age of rush, unending activity, and sound? John Wesley's mother raised ten children. It was when she covered her head with her apron that the children knew to leave her alone in her quiet time. The Word cries out to us,

> *"Be still and know I am God!"* **Psalm 46:10 (NASB)**

> *"Step out of the traffic! Take a long, loving look at Me, your high God, above politics, above everything else."* **Psalm 46:10 (MSG)**

Winter silence

15
SCOTCH TAPE AND SCISSORS

1968 November-JOURNAL ENTRY– Tonight is the eve of our 15th wedding anniversary. These years have been rich and rewarding. $300 in the bank but our fidelity and faithfulness have paid 300 times over in dividends. We don't own our home but possess our souls. No earthly fortune but millionaires in the wealth of two children who love Christ and respect their parents. We've lived and loved to see God's promise come true. *"But first seek the kingdom of God and His righteousness and all these things shall be added unto you."* Matt. 6:33 (NASB)

We walked hand in hand exploring the old Potawatomi Inn, Angola, Indiana, where we spent our weekend honeymoon. We watched a squirrel eat a nut, then talked about the book I was planning to write. One dozen red roses delivered to the sweetest girl in the world. Indeed, the day of days!

2000 February- REFLECTION - Four and a half decades later, I've learned much more about Marilyn. She doesn't want money spent on flowers. She desires more attention to detail, "Bob, by now you shouldn't have to ask, 'Where are the scotch tape and scissors kept.'"

Stock markets come and go. The investment we've made in marriage and family continues to bear dividends at an unbelievable rate! Our two children, their precious mates, plus two beautiful granddaughters. We're enjoying family more than ever before.

16
FAMILY

1971 March-JOURNAL ENTRY- What a joy our home has become. Marilyn served a delightful breakfast. It's always good to stop talking and listen. After breakfast, I made car repairs – new muffler and shocks. Then, I went shopping, and again the joy to sit and visit. My travel schedule was full. A call came in at 11:00 pm from a church in Missouri. They were looking for a preacher and asked me to consider.

March 20 - What a memorable evening! It began with a game of catch with my eleven-year-old daughter and fourteen-year-old son. Later, we changed the oil of my car, and my daughter got in the act. She loves to help; she insists she can do anything we can. "Daddy, it's fun to be dirty and greasy." Agreed. It's been a while since we spent real together time.

2016 September – REFLECTION - Life is what happens to you while you are busy doing something else. Our daughter and son-in-law are proud and loving grandparents. Our son and his wife will be married 35 years next week. In the midst of work, travel, daily pressure and unanswered questions about the election, we need to stop, think, and give thanks.

In 1971, cable TV, cell phones, texting, and Facebook were all non-existent. Calls were returned at one's convenience. People learned to wait. Often, by the time we could call back, the emergency had passed. Now we have another emergency called FAMILY. My family energizes me, but technology takes it away. I took our three great-grandsons fishing. Our youngest played with the worms while the two older ones were excited as they caught big ones! The cry of the hour, "I need someone to believe in, someone who will keep their word and be there for me."

> *"And now, God, do it again – bring rains into our drought-stricken lives so those who planted their crops in despair will shout hurrahs at the harvest, so those who went off with heavy hearts will come home laughing, with armloads of blessings."*
> **Psalm 126:4-6 (MSG)**

Bob at Grandpa Kern's farm

17
PREACHERS AS PERSUADERS

1972 April-JOURNAL ENTRY- Elton Trueblood spoke to me again in his book, *The New Man for our time*. "No experience is valid unless it leads to acts of justice and mercy." Christians are asked to combine the basin and the towel with the bread and wine. However, "It is a serious mistake to seek the change of the environment without also changing the man." He speaks to the need in our day, "To be truly modern, pay the price of rigorous thinking, and if we preachers want results, go beyond the guitars and contemporary music to the exciting truth."

People must first be convinced. I talked with one of our men who was upset with his wife. He wanted to run away, get drunk, and take out a woman. I counseled him to begin his thinking by first centering on Christ. Christ is not vague; He is a Person, God in the flesh. After our conversation, he decided to go home and talk things out with his wife.

April 2014 – REFLECTION - The needs of our day are no different. Preachers need to be persuaders! People need to be convinced more than ever of Jesus' identity and how He relates to this age.

Ravi Zacharias claims the need of the hour is for truth and relevance. We must begin where people are and relate to their need. Pleading a relevant answer in Christ changes one from despair and darkness to hope and light. But it must apply to the thinking and acting of our day.

The passing of time tests the relevance of valuable writing. Elton Trueblood stands as one of my earlier mentors.

"Jesus Christ is the same, yesterday and today and forever!" **Heb. 13:8 (NASB)**

18
THE ONLY RELIGION WITH A CROSS!

1972 APRIL 26-JOURNAL ENTRY- Trueblood spoke to me again in his chapter, 'Life of Service.' "No experience is valid unless it leads to acts of justice and mercy. Christians are asked to combine the basin and the towel with the bread and the wine." However, "it is a serious mistake to seek change of the environment without also changing the man."

"To be truly modern, pay the price of rigorous thinking, and if we preachers want results, go beyond the guitars and contemporary music to the exciting truth." He sees pastors as arousers of conviction. However, people must first be convinced. The place to begin in our thinking is with Christ. He is not vague. He is a Person. God in the flesh.

2017 Good Friday - REFLECTION (45 yrs. Later) - Ravi Zachariah often speaks at major universities and colleges. He always includes the cross of Christ. When he reaches that part of the story, dead silence follows. How could an innocent man suffer for the wrongs of others? He explains, "Christianity is the only religion with a cross. Buddha, before he died, admitted he was still searching for truth, and there is no cross in the Muslim story." Only Jesus could say, *"I am the way, and the truth and the life; no one comes to the Father, but through Me."* John 14:16 (NASB)

His name *is* Christ Jesus! *"HE IS RISEN! HE IS RISEN INDEED!"*

> *"But realize this, that in the last days, difficult times will come. For men will be lovers of self, money, boastful, arrogant, revilers, brutal, haters of good...lovers of pleasure rather than lovers of God. Therefore, let us run with endurance the race set before us. Fixing our eyes on Jesus!"* **2 Tim. 3:1-3, Hebrews 12:1-2 (NASB)**

Church of the Cross, Bradenton, Florida

19
PRAYER MEANS EVERYTHING

May 1972-JOURNAL ENTRY- What a joy to travel about the country sharing the good news of God's Spirit with fellow ministers. Today, I am going to Sydney, Ohio. Recently, I was told, "You have a circuit from Washington D.C. to St. Louis, Missouri, only you fly instead of riding a horse." I thank the Lord for this growing ministry to ministers.

How these men need encouragement and uplift. I led the minister's group in Sydney, beginning with "Growth by Groups" workshop. Each man was given I Corinthians 13 to paraphrase in his own understanding. Then as personal needs were shared, they formed small groups of three and prayed for one another by name. It was rich. In closing, I presented the vision of Key 73, reaching the continent for Christ that year. They listened with great interest and enthusiasm!

February 2008 – REFLECTION - Twenty-six years ago, volunteers in Key 73 outreach distributed the one volume Luke/Acts house-to-house in many major U.S. and Canadian cities. Denominations worked together as never before in that century. Church bells from coast to coast rang in the New Year as one of massive evangelism effort. Scores of denominations overcame pride and turf wars. Windows opened through many formerly closed walls. Many looked beyond their own "closed ranks" to discover that other Christians actually existed out there.

In 1997, I retired from the Broadway Christian Church in Fort Wayne, Indiana, as their preaching minister. For the past 11 years, I have been a pastor to pastors in the area of prayer. Our ministry was formerly known as "Prayer-A-Grams" for 28 years. The name was changed to "Pastors In Prayer" but with the same Board of Directors.

The needs of pastors and wives have accelerated this past decade. One estimate shows that only one in ten spiritual leaders finish strong. Prayers on our behalf mean everything. At times, we are told, "I pray for you and your work every day!" Every Christian worker crucially needs that level of commitment. Our passion finish strong!

"Every morning, You'll hear me at it again.
Every morning, I lay out the pieces of my life
on Your altar, and watch for the fire to descend."
Psalm 5:3 (MSG)

20
DAYS OF PRAYER

1973 October-JOURNAL ENTRY- This morning, I found myself in the empty, deserted sanctuary of the old Wayne St. UMC church building. Mayor Ivan Lebamoff spoke earlier that day at a minister's breakfast. He challenged us with a vision for the future. In Fort Wayne, he emphasized "downtown." The mayor addressed the need for a center of great potential and influence in the city because businesses and churches were leaving for the Suburbs.

This meeting led me to contemplate the potential of the deserted sanctuary and two-story education unit at Broadway and Wayne. I passed there earlier in the day. The owner of the building is asking for $150,000. This building is equipped and partially being used as a neighborhood center.

We are struggling with a building that seats 250 while there is nothing in sight for our future. Somehow, God seems to be leading me toward a preaching ministry there. "Lord, I am abiding tonight."

2011 October – REFLECTION - That unforgettable day, 38 years ago this week, is etched in my memory. I returned home unable to talk. My wife thought I'd been in an accident. Later that evening, we took a walk.

"Marilyn, I have seen a vision or dreamed a dream, not sure which." Her reply caught me off guard, "Bob, I told you two weeks ago when we drove by that building, we should consider buying it!" I did not recall hearing her, but Mother from the back seat confirmed the statement.

Having preached at the North Highlands Church for ten years, we were planning to build a $900,000 sanctuary in the suburbs. In 1973, the economy took a serious downturn. As the bank was approached for our promised loan, that amount was no longer available. We faced a brick wall of disappointment.

A small group had been praying at 5:30 a.m. for 38 days prior to the mayor's challenge. Months later, as the Lord led, we purchased the building for $125,000! Today, the congregation of Broadway Christian Church stands strong, preaching Christ in the central city.

Jesus once reminded His followers, ***"At all times they ought to pray and not lose heart."***
Luke 18:1 (NASB)

Broadway Christian Church, Ft. Wayne, Indiana

21
PARENTING IS TEMPORARY

1974 AUGUST 25-JOURNAL ENTRY- 7:45 p.m. This was a day of mixed emotions. I thought I was ready to leave my son at Milligan College, Tennessee, but found that the closer we came to saying goodbye, the harder I fought back the tears. I drove 50 miles while crying on the inside, with an occasional tear on the outside. In my mind, he is ready; he has proved himself.

SEPTEMBER 11 – I went to the garage this evening and saw everything in order. I've always wanted this, but when the kids were younger, they scattered things all over the place. But today, it hit me. They are about gone. My daughter is away for the weekend. I now have an orderly garage. I think I'd rather have it messed up!

2000 OCTOBER 11 – REFLECTION - Marilyn's fingerprints linger on each of these reflections. You may not see them, but let me tell you, she is one tough editor. "Bob, you must keep it brief, crisp, to the point, and always honest." In reflecting on the above, she reminded me, "Remember, parenting is temporary." She awoke on Sunday morning with the thought, "We did our best to raise our children to be independent. Our goal was to have them make it on their own and not be dependent on us. They know we will always be there for them."

What we experienced as parents was normal and necessary. We worked through the emotions of separation as the weeks and months passed. Two years later, our son arrived back home for a short time. He left a teenager; he returned an adult! It was hard for us at times because we still pictured him as he used to be. We soon realized that life together would never be the same. Thank You, Lord, that it wouldn't. It was time for us to let go, release him as our parents did to us. It was time for him to have his own life. Parenting may be temporary, but marriage is permanent!

> *"Point your kids in the right direction; when they're old, they won't be lost."* **Prov. 22:6 (MSG)**

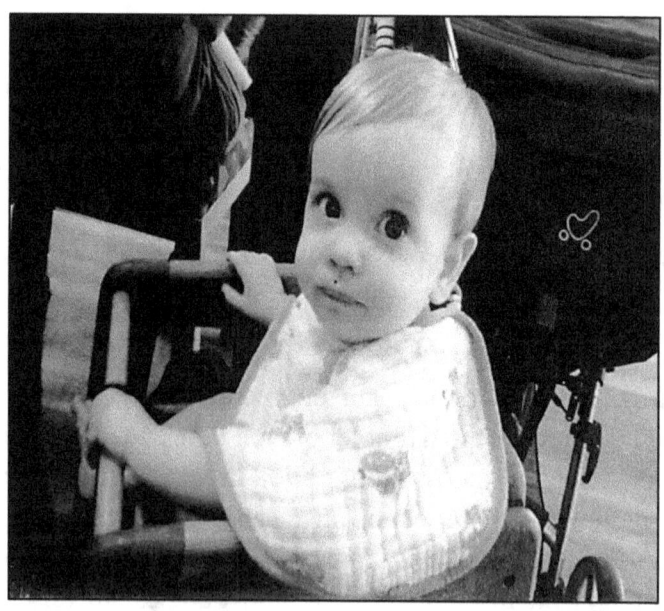

Youngest Great-grandson, Benjamin

22
ON RETREAT

1974 February-JOURNAL ENTRY- *"Not by might nor by power, but by My Spirit says the Lord of Hosts."* **Zachariah 4:6 (NASB)**

We sat by the window looking out over the snow-covered lake. After meditating on the promise from the prophet Zachariah, we formed a circle and began to look inward. I observed, "The lake out our window is partly frozen. A warm sun will thaw it soon. How like that we are, frozen yet thawing a little around the edges, but in need of God's warm Son to shine on us and melt our spirits." And He did!

Through praise and song, prayer for one another, we turned to the person on our left, telling them of our love and why we cared. We were on a retreat at Winona Lake, Indiana, in the old hotel. Soon, we had our arms around one another, with tears flowing and the Holy Spirit melting our hearts. What a joy. One man said, "This was the most relaxing and Spirit-led retreat I have ever been on."

2008 March – REFLECTION - The author, Esther de Waal, in a *Seven Day Journey with Thomas Merton* (1993), states, "It's time to stop running in all the different directions that seemed so attractive and instead take time to be." In quoting Merton, De Wall added, "Today, time is a commodity, and for each of us, time is mortgaged… we must approach the whole idea of time in a new way." Merton adds in *New Seeds of Contemplation* (1961), "As long as we are on earth, the love that unites us will bring us suffering by our very contact with one another because this love is the resetting of a Body of broken "bones.""

23
WORTH THE WAIT!

1974 May-JOURNAL ENTRY- I am facing a personal paradox over the Lausanne, Switzerland, Meeting. Before the Broadway Church started in January, I was registered for the first such international evangelism gathering. But now, my time spent in starting the new work is vital in Fort Wayne, Indiana. I believe it is more pleasing to the Lord for me to do evangelism during this first summer than attend a conference about it.

My great-grandfather, Jon Hans Yawberg, came from near Berne, Switzerland, sometime in the 1850s. How I yearn to visit the land of his birth. But there is a reality check in my spirit. This is not the time.

2011 December 29 – REFLECTION – In the summer of 1974, I visited nearly every home and apartment between the old West Wayne UMC Church building and the St Joe River. Since that building housed the newly established Broadway Christian Church, it was vital to invite the old West Central neighborhood to the new congregation at the corner of Broadway and Wayne. My goal was unchanged: to preach Christ to the central city of Fort Wayne.

Twenty-three years later, Marilyn and I could hardly process what we heard on the evening of our retirement and commissioning. Hundreds gathered on one of the coldest nights of 1997. Our elder chairman narrated the slide show, explaining the expansive trip about to be given. Could he possibly be saying, "An all-expense paid trip to Germany and Switzerland?"

John and Sue Drummond (my secretary and husband) volunteered to accompany us since John did business near the little village of my great-grandfather's birth. Was it worth waiting 23 years? Yes, many times over. Had we gone in 1974, I would have been alone and spent the week inside a convention hall. God is faithful! He gave me the desires of my heart. First, in establishing the Broadway Church, and second, in His time, visiting the birthplace of my ancestors.

"Take delight in the LORD, and He will give you your heart's desires." **Psalm 37:4 (NLT)**

Spietz, Switzerland

24
I PULLED THE WEED

1976 June-JOURNAL ENTRY- On my morning walk, a colorful page on the sidewalk caught my eye. Reaching down to pick it up, I found myself holding a page torn from a porn magazine. Suddenly, spiritual warfare marred the beauty of this June morning.

Opening my New Testament in the other hand to **Romans 12:1 (NASB), "I urge you, therefore, brethren by the mercies of God, to *present your bodies a living and holy sacrifice, acceptable to God. Do not be conformed to this world but be transformed by the renewing of your mind."*** The young woman posing in that photo offered her body to the evil one and his intentions.

Approaching our driveway, I noticed a tiny morning glory weed stretched over my rock garden. What about the garden of my mind? Sin chokes good thoughts or good thoughts choke sin. I pulled the weed and tore up the porn page.

2017August – REFLECTION - My youngest granddaughter gave me a small book one Christmas: Gods Promises for Men. Walking on the treadmill last winter, I meditated on these Bible promises, one short verse at a time. It's amazing how they come to mind at unexpected times and stay with me. *"Delight yourself in the Lord, and He will give you the desires of your heart."* **Psalm 37:4 (NASB)**

In what do I delight? What are the desires of my heart? "Two natures beat within my breast. One is foul, the other blessed. The one I love, the other I detest. The one I feed will dominate."

"Father, please protect and empower us as we seek to resist temptation in this sexually perverted culture. We offer ourselves as a sacrifice. May we be pleasing to You and a blessing to our families. In Jesus Name, Amen."

World Magazine reports, **"68% of Christian men view porn on a regular basis... the hardest part is pornography's effect on relationships with God, spouses and other people. There's no reprieve... it really owns you."**

Bridge over St. Mary's River

25
WHY DADDY, WHY?

1976 November (Thanksgiving Day) - JOURNAL ENTRY- "Why, Daddy? Why? Why? Why does God let Grandpa be like we found him today?" We were returning from the Hillcrest Nursing Home where we watched them feed him dinner. He seemed to recognize us when we first arrived, but then went on eating as if we were not there. I drove back the tears. It's now been three months since his massive stroke.

2011 November- REFLECTION - My answer to a tearful daughter came as we walked near Dad's home. "God uses suffering to prepare us, to help us not get too attached to this world. We forget what He has prepared for us yet to come."

The answer seemed so simple. But two years later, I found my father with two bed sores (no lack of loving care by his nurse and my faithful Mom). I too was asking the same question again. Why Lord? He was a Godly man, married 50 years to the same woman. Why, why? Could it be that the Lord was reminding a little girl and her father of His promise? *"And if I go and prepare a place for you, I will come again and receive you to Myself, that where I am, there you may be also."* **John 14:3 (NASB)**

His passing came on a Thursday morning, with Mom and Marilyn at his bedside. I read the Psalms; we sang the old hymns. Mother had not witnessed a death before then. "I never knew anyone could die so peacefully!" she exclaimed. "Mom," I replied, "When our Lord Jesus took him into His arms, Dad had final peace."

"Peace I leave with you, My peace I give to you; not as the world gives, do I give to you. Let not your heart be troubled, nor let it be afraid." **John 14:27 (NASB)**

26
LEAD GENTLY

1977 August-JOURNAL ENTRY- Words from an elder's wife:

"Bob must be strong and wise and lead differently. He must lead gently." The phrase "lead gently" kept coming back to me.

She continued, "We must strive to keep in contact with all our present members, teach them personally if need be, call on them and help them to understand that there is so much more to learn and experience in God and Jesus and the Spirit."

2018 February – REFLECTION - Those words, I've never forgotten. The Broadway Church was but four years old. Her members had been leaving for numerous reasons. Some moved to other cities; others complained that we were moving too fast; some were just not ready for the culture of downtown Fort Wayne, Indiana.

Phyllis and her husband, George, stood firmly with us in the most difficult of times. What a sharp mind and caring spirit this lady exemplified. Today, she is with the Lord. Those words penned on the flyleaf of my Bible 41 years ago, come back often as a reminder. "Lead gently."

Jesus called His followers, "sheep." He knew how often sheep stray, one going over a cliff may lead others to the same fate. Leadership is costly. Leadership requires listening, as well as speaking. Above all, it requires listening to the Holy Spirit through God's Word.

"The mark of a good leader is loyal followers; leadership is nothing without a following." **Proverbs 14:28 (MSG)**

27
MY DAD TAUGHT ME

1977 November-JOURNAL ENTRY– I was scheduled to meet in Indy with several preachers from across the state, but I wasn't feeling well, so I canceled. Instead, I spent two hours with one of our young men who wanted to be discipled.

He observed being with me in a number of different settings had helped him know how to be a man. We stopped once to help a young mother and baby near her stranded VW. Later, he watched as we ministered to two sisters who had just lost their mother to death.

This past week, I was with a young man who said to me, "I saw how a man takes charge and leads, and you did that. Another time in a restaurant, you paid the bill for your family. I want to pay the bill this a.m.; I need to do that." What a humbling experience. We influence people most when realizing it the least. Discipleship is caught as much as taught.

2011 October – REFLECTION - Who is a man? What does he look like? For me, it was my father. What did I learn from Dad? He taught me to work and stay with a job — he worked for 42 years at the same factory. He taught me the importance of loving one woman in a lifetime — he was married to Mom for over 50 years.

He taught me to hunt and fish, take a vacation, plant and harvest a garden, ride a bike and drive the '37 Willys. Together, we tried out our first speedboat (Evinrude outboard) on the Maumee River, a rooster tail of white water behind us.

Most of all, he taught me to love Jesus. I never heard him take the Lord's name in vain. He took his family to church every Sunday. I still have the hand-written letter he sent when I was away at college. "Remember, Bob. Still water runs deep." My Dad taught me how to be a man.

> *"How blessed is the man who does not walk in the counsel of the wicked…His delight is in the law of the Lord…He will be like a tree firmly planted by streams of water which yields its fruit in its season."* **Psalm 1 (NASB)**

Bob with his father

28
WORSHIP STYLE

1978 September-JOURNAL ENTRY– Tonight, at an elders' meeting, the question was asked, "Why do we have 250 this September when there were 350 attending a year ago?" Our worship leader, Pat Black, and I were exhorted to be sure we follow the Lord's leading. How can we be sure we are responding to the Lord? Be sensitive to where He would lead.

I don't know where we are just now, yet I believe I am following the Lord's direction; I wait and listen.

2015 March – REFLECTION - Worship style has become the battleground in many local churches! Traditional vs. contemporary, hymns vs. "choruses" and scripture songs.

Which is best? Which is right? Neither, if one or the other causes division in Christ's body. I well remember the comments of an older saint when we introduced the "new" worship in the early 80s. He wisely noted, "More and more young people are attending and if that brings them in, I'm for it!"

Lest we forget, it's not about us. It's all about Jesus! How we worship should never get in the way of whom we worship.

Pat Black once wrote, "Know the dominant age group and cultural orientation of those you lead. Learn to be flexible and versatile." Lest we forget, "**Even *the Son of Man did not come to be served, but to serve and give His life a ransom for many.*** Mark 10:45 (NASB).** Avoid the kind of professionalism that insists on only doing your thing. Be a servant!

29
MILKWEED PODS IN THE WIND

1980 October-JOURNAL ENTRY- On retreat. I didn't realize how much I needed this time away. I've been deeply affected by several families leaving of late. One lady counted 24 families this past year — 14 moved out of town and 9 to other ministries. Some didn't understand the direction of discipleship. A finance sheet was passed out, showing unpaid bills of $3,400. A few responded. God's spiritual resources remain unlimited!

Finally, I took a walk to Golden maples and scarlet oaks, across from Highland Cemetery. Cold wind but radiant sky where the sun's searching rays broke through the overcast. I waved a bursting milkweed pod over my head and watched the wind scatter ripe seeds across the scrub growth, each with its tiny parachute. Two deer crashed through the underbrush. The feelings were finally returning.

Paul asks, *"Have you ever come on anything quite like this extravagant generosity of God, this deep wisdom?*

Everything comes from Him;
Everything happens through Him;
Everything ends up in Him.
Always glory! Always praise! YES, YES, YES."
Romans 11:33 (MSG)

2000 October – REFLECTION - Leadership training appears as the main priority today for pastors' preparation. Leadership apart from spiritual formation leaves a great void. "Spiritual formation focuses on the internal aspects of faith, such as the fruit of the Spirit and prayer. Pastors need to know how to grow spiritually in their own lives as well as how to lead others to do the same." – *Christianity Today* pastors, Back to Basics, Fall 2017

Periodic retreats gave me time away to pray and get back in touch with the Lord. I need vital time to meditate in the Word for my own soul's sake, and more walks in October to rediscover God's indiscernible creation, milkweed pods, and deer.

30
SOLITUDE

1981 January-JOURNAL ENTRY- I arrived for a monthly retreat following our study in *Celebration of Discipline* by Richard Foster. It's a struggle to leave home in the evening, and tonight is no exception. Yet, once I get away, it's always worth it. Solitude is not a luxury; it's a necessity!

Foster writes, "Four times a year, withdraw for three to four hours to reorient your life goals. Find a quiet place away from your daily distractions. What do you want to have accomplished one year from now? Be willing to dream, to stretch. Keep a journal record of what comes to you."

2007 November – REFLECTION - There are times when God is very silent. Such times mean patient obedience and keeping busy with the task at hand. Active waiting!

Jesus often spent alone time with the Father. In solitude, He prayed and sought the Father's will. From there, He went out to gather the results of His prayers. John records these words of our Lord, *"I do nothing on my own initiative, but I speak these things as the Father taught me. And he who sent me is with me; He has not left me alone, for I always do the things that are pleasing to him."* **John 8:28-29 (NASB)**

Maumee River, Grand Rapids, Ohio (Marilyn's home)

31
REPENTANCE AND HOLINESS

1983 June-JOURNAL ENTRY- Billy Graham Center, Wheaton, ILL. – Reading from A. Wallis, *In The Day of Thy Power*: "The way to a revived church is still repentance and true holiness!" Why do we not pray for another great revival, day and night? Could it be because we have never really known such a time or believe it could be in this day and age? Coming to realize that 125 years have passed since the last countrywide outpouring (prayer meeting revival of 1858 when business men prayed on their knees; the week NY City banks failed). It has been over 150 years since the Second Great Awakening with Charles Finney. "Certainly, the time is due, past due, and yet the church is not ready!" Am I ready? That's the real question.

2009 November – REFLECTION - Revival can be defined as "returning to our first love with Christ Jesus." In the early 1980s, I preached 132 sermons on the theme of "Revival-Spiritual Awakening!" It was during that series, Charlotte (our spiritual mentor and prayer partner) noted, "I have always been for balance, but as revival comes, we won't have it. We'll have to get over hurrying away to dinner with our 5 or 6 people because the Spirit will have us stay with the body for a much longer time."

History can teach us if only we will take the time to learn and realize our previous conditions, which brought the Lord's sustained presence and blessing. Repentance and holiness have not gone out of date, just out of style.

> *"I know your deeds, and your toil and perseverance...you have endured for My name's sake, and have not grown weary. But I have this against you, that you have left your first love. Remember therefore from where you have fallen and repent and do the deeds you did at first; or else I am coming to you and will remove your lampstand out of its place---unless you repent."* **Rev. 2:2-5 (NASB)**

32
URGENT OR IMPORTANT

1984 March-JOURNAL ENTRY– This was another test day in the porn battle. I got a call came from an unnamed person. He offered the sale of the building formerly housing the Erotica House porn pit. He thought the purchase could be made for $135,000.

I was excited. At once, I looked upon it as an answer to many prayers. However, after further prayer for discernment, the caller rang again a few days later. "The owner is tipsy now," he warned. All at once, I became suspicious. One of our elders had told me earlier, "the urgent is not usually important; the truly important is not urgent, give it a couple of days." The caller insisted on $10,000 down.

1993 March – REFLECTION - Nine long years later, the building went on the market; we bid $57,350. The realtor wanted more. We held firm and learned later that ours was the only bid.

My lifelong problem has been acting on impulse. By praying more, much more, and listening to wise counsel, God's final answer emerged. In one offering, our congregation generously provided the price.

Thirty-four (34) years later, at that same location, the *In-As-Much Ministry* gave spiritual and physical assistance to the less fortunate. Thirty-one (31) area congregations provided volunteers and finances from that location.

**"I was hungry, and you fed Me,
I was thirsty, and you gave Me a drink,
I was homeless, and you gave Me a room,
I was shivering, and you gave Me clothes,
I was sick, and you stopped to visit,**

I was in prison, and you came to Me."

Matt. 25:35-36 (MSG)

"Inasmuch as ye have done it unto one of the least of these my brethren, ye have done it unto Me." 25:40 (KJV)

33
DISCIPLE-MAKING

1985 March-JOURNAL ENTRY-

1. "Beware of bringing out a truth before you have developed it." - D. Prince

2. "Ten men acting together can make a hundred thousand tremble apart from each other." - Crosier House Retreat, Mirabeau.

3. "When you make a big decision of faith, you can build on it for a lifetime." - Ernie Chamberlin

4. "If we answer the call to discipleship, where will it lead us? It matters not where, I can but follow Him." - Bonhoeffer

2012 June – REFLECTION - How have these principles affected my life? I paid dearly when bringing out a truth too soon. Like a Roman candle on the fourth of July, it shot up brightly, drew lots of attention but plummeted to ashes. Over and over, "discipleship" has remained a burning truth and vision. May I never forget Jesus' clear command, *"Go therefore and make disciples…"* **Matt. 28:19 (NASB)**

All too often, preachers want hundreds if not thousands. While at that very moment, two or three are anxiously waiting to be discipled! Jesus spent three years investing Himself in 12 men. Later, He increased the circle to 70. At the time of His death, 120 assembled for prayer in the upper room. Not until Pentecost were 3,000 baptized.

> *"So, my son, throw yourself into this work for Christ. Pass on what you heard from me… to reliable leaders who are competent to teach others. When the going gets tough, take it on the chin with the rest of us, the way Jesus did."* **2 Timothy 2:1-3 (MSG)**

Oldest Great-grandson, Brody

34
SECOND SOPRANO

1992 March-JOURNAL ENTRY- As we were eating at the MCL Cafeteria, Marilyn described herself as a "Second Soprano." I kept what she wrote on a napkin. "There's no melody to send out, very monotonous to most. Never soaring to a soprano's breathtaking emotional high, not reaching the amazing alto depths of study and intellect – just filling in the gaps to cover their weaker moments so that harmony and balance can prevail." Second soprano was the part she sang for many years in her ladies' trio.

2017 August – REFLECTION - This SYG is dedicated to pastor's wives everywhere. Marilyn became one at 18, the day she said "I do" to me. She accepted that task after much prayer. By nature, she has always been one to work behind the scenes, exercising her gifts to helping and serving.

In our last ministry in the central city of Fort Wayne, Indiana, her role changed to overseeing the nursery after the church found an organist to replace her. The Lord then led her to the door. What a door, as people from all walks of life entered from city streets. First time folk always greeted with a smile and welcoming hand. She made a point of remembering to call them by name on the very next visit.

The "First Lady" as she is respectfully known in many black congregations, is often one of the loneliest in the church. There may be none to turn to when her husband is falsely criticized - no one, that is, but the Lord. These dear ladies are the special angels of mercy. Fellow-pastor, pray often with and for your precious wife. The same goes for all who pass her every Sunday. Let her know by word, letter, email, or text how very much she means to your family and church.

> *"A good woman is hard to find, and her worth is far more than diamonds. Her husband trusts her without reserve, and never has reason to regret it... Many women have done wonderful things, but you've outclassed them all!"* Prov. 31:10-11, 29 (MSG)

35
THE TIGHTROPE WALKER

1995 March-JOURNAL ENTRY- In the past, God has always led us, right at the very hour we needed Him. He never fails! If only we can quiet ourselves (if only I can) to hear His voice, prompting and leading. Charlotte, our mentor, once said, "The tightrope walker in the circus falls most often by taking the last three or four steps. This is because of too much confidence as he is ending his act."

I believe we face the most dangerous time of our entire ministry. "Success," whatever it is, however, men may define it, is dangerous. Lord, deliver me from pride, too much ego, from even thinking I have done anything. You, O Lord, are my all in all! Protect me from such a fall. How do I lead? And even more, where do I find the time to hear You, and once I have heard, then to follow?

2009 June – REFLECTION - Loren Cunningham, founder of Youth With A Mission, in his book, *Daring To Live On The Edge* (2004) tells how he uses Listening Prayers. "An impression in your spirit can only come from one of four sources; your own mind, the mind of others, the mind of Satan, or the mind of God. Use the example of ***"Submit therefore to God, Resist the devil, and he will flee from you."*** **James 4:7 (NASB)** to silence Satan and ***"taking every thought captive to the obedience of Christ,"*** **2 Cor. 10:5. (NASB)** God has given you the authority in Christ to silence the other sources and clear the way to hear and know it is God speaking. He further suggests writing whatever we hear and then obeying it without reservation since we know the word is from the Lord.

36
SHORTER PRAYERS

1995 December-JOURNAL ENTRY- Our two granddaughters are here for the night. We sit around the dining room table to play monopoly. I suggest we say prayers of thanksgiving before we start. The oldest speaks up (just like her mom used to), "Grandpa, that means short prayers not long sentences with lots of commas, only one line." As only she could put it, being such an avid reader and aware of language structure and grammar. Her sister agreed, so we prayed but kept it short.

2007 October – REFLECTION - Jesus prayed short prayers in public.

"When you pray, say..." **Luke 11:2-4 (NASB)** but spent the entire night **Luke 6:12 (NASB)** when alone with the Father. In solitude with the "Ancient of Days," He listened for direction. He left prayer and acted on what His Father directed by selecting the 12 Apostles.

Jesus went from prayer time and place to reap the results of His prayers. Let us pray first, be it alone, before a game of monopoly, preparing a sermon or lesson, or meeting with friends. Lord, what do You expect from this time we spend together?

"The first thing I want you to do is pray. Pray every way you know how, for everyone you know… This is the way our Savior God wants us to live." **1 Timothy 2:1a-1b (MSG)**

Our two Grand-daughters

37
DISCIPLESHIP IN TWO YEARS

1997 October-JOURNAL ENTRY- A very profitable morning as I worked over the sermon topics on Discipleship for the next two years! It's amazing how long it will take us, and yet not so long either. Anything worth doing is worth taking the time.

October 20 – I am committed to a few men, like never before. It means there is no turning back, no changing ministries, but simply going on and keeping faith with my Lord and these men and women. Lately, it seems we are at a standstill, or at least on a plateau. It's one thing to talk about community and commitment to one another in Christ. It's another to work it out nearby. This takes much love and patience, and it happens only as the Holy Spirit empowers and enables.

November 2009 – REFLECTION - Discipleship in two years? More like 20! The above was written in our fourth year of ministry at the Broadway Church. If it took our Lord three long years to disciple His men, why should we as pastors think we can do it in two or less? I still had a lot to learn, and I am still learning.

Today, around every corner stands someone hawking wisdom and goodness on easy terms. But this is not what history and experience teach. To the contrary, almost everything worth doing in human life is very difficult in its early stages.

"Think of all the resolutions we begin and never finish. Starting is easy. Following through is hard. We must submit ourselves knowing the rigors of discipline certainly lead to the easy yoke and the full joy of Christ." - Dallas Willard, *The Spirit of Disciplines*.

> *"All authority has been given to Me in heaven and on earth. 'Go therefore and make disciples of all the nations, baptizing them in the name of the Father and the Son and the Holy Spirit, teaching them to observe all that I commanded you; and lo, I am with you always, even to the end of the age."* **Matt. 28:18b-20 (NASB)**

Our son and daughter on the trail

38
BELOVED SUFFERER

1974 March-JOURNAL ENTRY- Turning 41; I don't find this birthday at all difficult. Turning 40 did evoke some serious thought. My major concern for the next decade of my life is to be "poured out for Him." Who and what and when He wants! The time is short. His coming must be close, and there's so much still to do. Sermons have been preached, lessons have been taught, and souls have been won! Oh, to say with John, "Even so come, Lord Jesus!"

2011 July – REFLECTION – Now, as I am only two years from 80, what was written at 41 seems very distant. Very few sermons or lessons taught, yet always more souls to be won and discipled. Our dual focus is His continual Presence and the hope of heaven. Ed Hayden best describes where Marilyn and I now find ourselves.

Beloved Sufferer
"When I no longer have
What I now enjoy,
May God give me the grace
To enjoy what I shall then have.

Since I no longer
Have some things
I once enjoyed,
May God give me the grace
To enjoy what I now have."

"There is an opportune time to do things, a right time for everything on the earth: The last and final word is this: Fear God. Do what He tells you. God will bring everything out into the open and judge it according to its hidden intent, whether it's good or evil."
Ecclesiastes 3:1, 12:13 (MSG)

Still saying, YES!

39
FROM FOUNTAIN PEN TO COMPUTER

1992 February-JOURNAL ENTRY- Holli, my eight-year-old granddaughter, leads her class in computer skills. She sat down and patiently instructed grandpa on how to use the "word processor." It's an old computer, the size of a small suitcase. Brent gave it to me when he no longer needed it in his office. On Friday, I was frustrated, but it got better tonight.

I must change with the times! It's hard; I'm more comfortable with my faithful "Schaeffer" fountain pen and a yellow tablet. I need to be stretched in learning how the modern world now communicates.

REFLECTION - APRIL 2016 - (24 years later). Change is still hard. The only thing in a culture that doesn't change is "change" itself. I remember saying 63 years ago that I would "never" live in the city, and within a few months, I was called to Fort Wayne, Indiana. Later, "Okay, the suburbs I can handle, but no more." Less than ten years passed, and God's call came again, this time to minister of all places, downtown Fort Wayne.

With the change from pen to hand-typed words came another call. In 1999, I prayed Matt. 7:7 asking, "Lord, what do You have for me, now semi-retired and facing a new millennium?" The answer soon came.

I looked over my journals which spanned 43 years (now 64), and I realized these pages contained the story of our life's struggles, joys, and heartaches. Known as all-consuming work (the ministry), what should I select? Will it be of any value? Who would read it? All these questions were answered with the first "Saying Yes to God" (SYG) sent January 6, 2000. These periodic emails reached worldwide to innumerable pastors, leaders, and friends. Thanks Holli, for teaching your ever-learning granddad how to transition from "Schaeffer" to "Apple."

> *"Ask, and it shall be given to you; seek and you will find, knock and it will be opened to you."* **Matt. 7:7 (NAS)**
>
> *"Jesus Christ is the same yesterday, today, and forever!"* **Hebrews 13:8 (LNT)**

Great-grandson, Braxton, our faith lives on.

40
"SOUL OF CHRIST"

Jesus, may all that is in you flow into me.
May your body and blood be my food and drink.
May your passion and death be my strength and life.
Jesus, with you by my side, enough has been given.
May the shelter I seek be the shadow of your cross.
Let me not run from the love which you offer.
But hold me safe from the forces of evil.
On each of my dying, shed your light and your love.
Keep calling to me until that day comes.
When with our saints, I may praise you forever.

- Fr. David L. Fleming, S.J.
(Translator of St. Ignatius)

www.ingramcontent.com/pod-product-compliance
Lightning Source LLC
Chambersburg PA
CBHW071411290426
44108CB00014B/1778